Measuring Time

Seasons of the Year

Tracey Steffora

Heinemann Library
Chicago, Illinois

www.capstonepub.com
Visit our website to find out more information about Heinemann-Raintree books.

To order:
Phone 800-747-4992
Visit www.capstonepub.com to browse our catalog and order online.

© 2011 Heinemann Library
an imprint of Capstone Global Library, LLC
Chicago, Illinois

All rights reserved. No part of this publication may be reproduced or transmitted in any form or by any means, electronic or mechanical, including photocopying, recording, taping, or any information storage and retrieval system, without permission in writing from the publisher.

Edited by Tracey Steffora and Dan Nunn
Designed by Richard Parker
Picture research by Hannah Taylor
Originated by Capstone Global Library Ltd

Library of Congress Cataloging-in-Publication Data
Steffora, Tracey.
Seasons of the year / Tracey Steffora.
p. cm.—(Measuring time)
Includes bibliographical references and index.
ISBN 978-1-4329-4902-0 (hc)—ISBN 978-1-4329-4909-9 (pb)
ISBN 978-1-4846-0083-2 (saddle stitch)
1. Seasons—Juvenile literature. 2. Time—Juvenile literature. 3. Time measuremet—Juvenile literature. I. Title.
QB637.4.S725 2011
508.2—dc22
2010028871

Acknowledgments
Alamy: Bob Handelman, cover bottom left, Christina Bollen, cover bottom right, Cultura, 4, David Noton Photography, cover top right, Jon Helgason, 22 middle, RubberBall, 15; Getty Images: JGI/Jamie Grill, 21, MIXA, cover top left, Thinkstock Images, 10; iStockphoto: David Safanda, 22 top, Ermin Gultenberger, back cover, 6, LeoGrand, 14, mammamaart, 22 bottom, Morley Read, 19, Primary Picture, 16; NASA: 23 top; Shutterstock: almgren, 7, Dennis W Donohue, 17, FotoYakov, 8, Graeme Dawes, 20, Nagel Photography, 11, oriontrail, 23 bottom, RazvanZinica, 12, Shebeko, 13, Supermop, 5; SuperStock: James Urbach, 18

Every effort has been made to contact copyright holders of any material reproduced in this book. Any omissions will be rectified in subsequent printings if notice is given to the publisher.

Printed in the United States 4995

Contents

Time and Seasons 4
Winter 10
Spring 12
Summer 14
Fall 16
Around the World 18
Picture Glossary 23
Index 24

Time and Seasons

Time is how long something takes.

Time is when things happen.

Some things take a short time.
Some things take a long time.

A season is a long amount of time.

There are four seasons in one year.

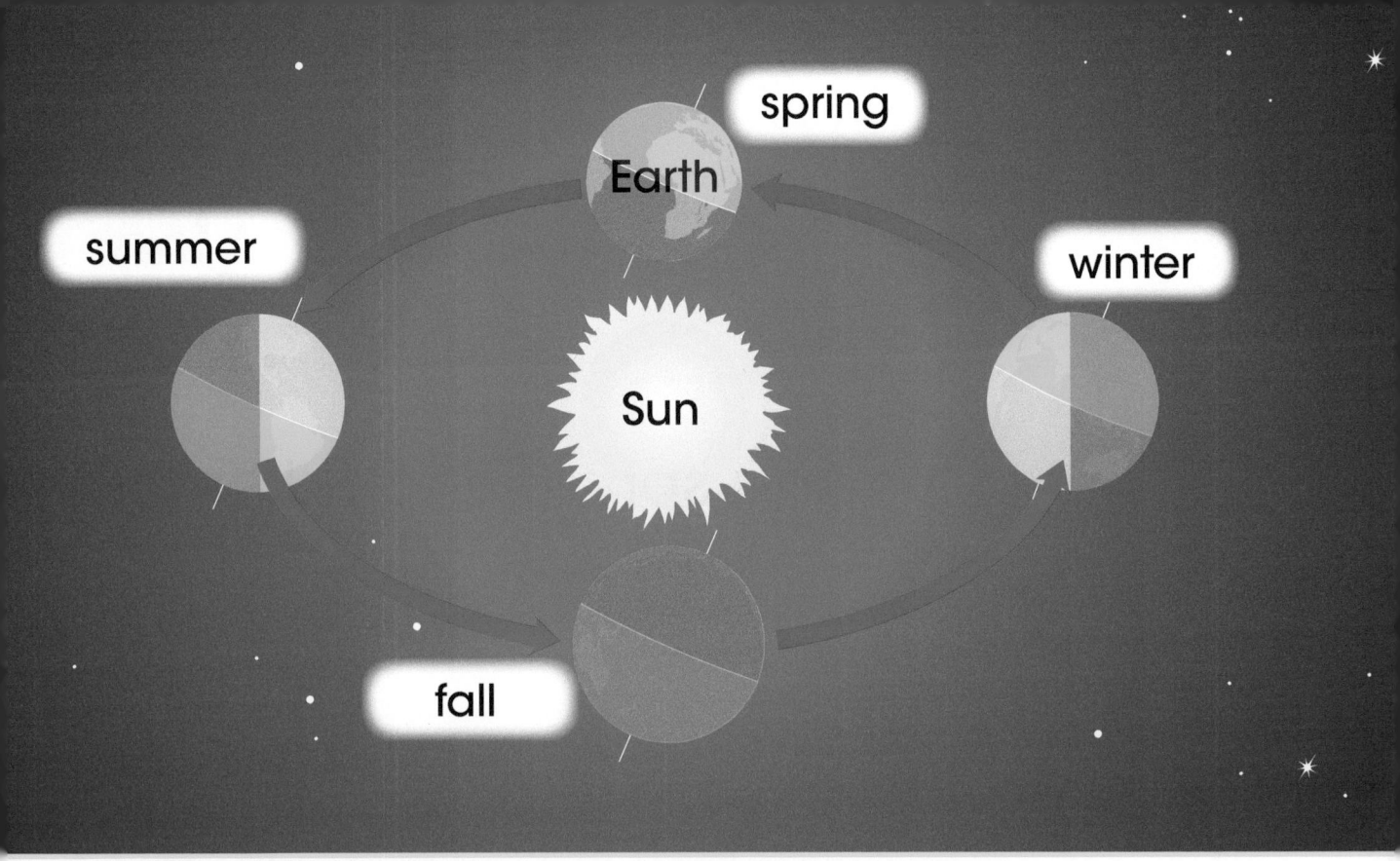

The seasons change as the Earth travels around the Sun.

Winter

In winter we feel the cold.

In winter we taste hot chocolate.

In winter we hear the wind.

In winter we see bare trees.

Spring

In spring we feel warm weather.

In spring we hear birds sing.

In spring we see new plants.

In spring we smell flowers.

Summer

In summer we feel the heat.

In summer we see the bright Sun.

In summer we taste fresh berries.

In summer we hear water splash.

Fall

In fall we feel cool air.

In fall we hear leaves crunch.

In fall we feel a warm sweater.

In fall we see birds flying south.

In fall we see leaves change color.

Around the World

Some places are always cold.

Some places are always hot.

We use a calendar to know the season.

see hear feel taste smell

We use our senses to know the season.

What are the seasons like where you live?

Picture Glossary

Earth the planet on which we live

Sun the star that gives heat and light to the Earth; the Earth travels around the Sun

Index

Earth 9
fall 8, 9, 16, 17
spring 8, 9, 12, 13
summer 8, 9, 14, 15
Sun 9, 14
winter 8, 9, 10, 11

Note to Parents and Teachers

Before reading

Discuss the current season and characteristics of that season where you live. Prompt children to think about the different clothing they might wear during different seasons. Review the five senses with children and begin a discussion of things that they see, hear, smell, feel, and taste each season.

After reading

- Collect photos that illustrate different seasons and use as a sorting activity.
- You might explain to children that a season also refers to a certain time of year that is characterized by a particular event or activity (e.g., strawberry season, football season, allergy season). Encourage them to name and identify other seasons with which they are familiar.